A Prayer Pal a Day
Keeps me Moving God's way

31 Prayer Pals for Vibrant Living

By Beth Rudy

A Prayer Pal A Day Keeps Me Moving God's Way
Published by Beth Rudy

©2013 by Beth Rudy
ISBN: 978-0-9894718-1-7

Cover Design by Nancy Sebastian Meyer
Copy Editor Nancy Sebastian Meyer

For information:
PRAYER PAL, 2516 STATE STREET, EAST PETERSBURG, PA 17520

Dedication

Pastor Claire and Carlene Harstad inspired me to identify my God-given purpose in life, and then exercise faith and overcome fear of failure to fulfill it.

My purpose is to glorify God, magnify Jesus Christ, and proclaim and explain biblical principles for vibrant living.

Introduction

A Prayer Pal a Day Keeps Me Moving God's Way is the second in a series of short Prayer Pal™ devotional books intended to build up the Church, the beautiful Bride of Christ, in preparation for His return. He is coming! Are you ready?

For many years, I tried adding Jesus to my religion and my lifestyle. I didn't appreciate His value. I wasn't fascinated by His character. Nor was I captivated by the Cross. Tossing Him aside like a temporal treasure, I spent 20 years in the rat race where the pace was set by the world. My only reward was exhaustion and entrapment.

Worn out and burned out by empty religion and endless activity, I began seeking something more – God. In my quest to discover Him, the Holy Spirit led me to Henry Blackaby's, *Experiencing God.* Through the Word of God, the Bible, I become completely captivated by Christ and mesmerized by the Cross. As a discipline, I learned to read, reflect, and respond to His precepts, principles and promises with love letters from my heart.

A few years later, revival services came to my church. We were challenged to find a "Spiritual Pal" for accountability. Mine was my best friend, Ann with whom I shared my love letters to God. She dubbed me "Prayer Pal" and encouraged me to publish them.

Prayer Pal™ has been published since 2005 via email and internet as a witness of God's love and faithfulness. Thousands of readers all over the world find my Prayer Pals eloquently express their own heart toward God.

Jesus said, "The thief's purpose is to steal and kill and destroy. My purpose is to give them a rich and satisfying life." John 10:10.

Since prayer helps us grow closer to God and experience a more vibrant relationship with Him, I have published this little book that you can carry in your pocket, your brief case, or your car to keep you moving God's way—in His direction and according to His will.

May the prayers from my heart bless your heart!

All for the King!

Beth

Day One

The Gift of Salvation

John 3:16-17

For God loved the world so much that he gave his one and only Son, so that everyone who believes in him will not perish but have eternal life. God sent his Son into the world not to judge the world, but to save the world through him.

Jesus, My Savior,

I BELIEVE You are the One and Only Son of God sent into the world as a generous gift from above to reconcile me with God for all eternity. Receiving You by faith guarantees that my life will be recreated, my days will be redeemed, and my relationship with Him will be restored forever.

No matter how monstrously I've messed up, I don't have to fear future punishment. Blessed assurance!

> M-y
> E-vil has been
> R-econciled by
> C-hrist's
> Y-ielding

Thank You for the incredible gift of my salvation bought with Your precious, priceless blood that was shed for me on Calvary. By Your grace and with faith, I gratefully accept You as Lord of my life and my Eternal Savior. Amen.

This is the truth: Salvation is God's gift to You. Have you accepted it? God absolutely loves YOU. When you confess that you are a sinner, God forgives you completely forever, freeing you to get up and go LIVE vibrantly in Him and with others.

Day Two

Complete in Christ

Colossians 2:10

So you also are complete through your union with Christ, who is the head over every ruler and authority.

Jesus,

I BELIEVE You reign supreme and that I am complete in You. When I accepted Your extravagant gift of salvation, You performed a miraculous change in my heart by cutting away my old, nasty nature. Buried with You through baptism, I was also raised with You to an exciting new life, because I trusted the mighty power of God that raised You from the dead.

I BELIEVE I am alive with You, forgiven and free because You cancelled all the charges against me and took them away by nailing them to the cross.

I BELIEVE I am victorious because You disarmed the dirty devil and his slippery sidekicks, publicly disgracing them when You triumphed over the grave. Because I am united with You, sin no longer has a grip on me.

Since there is NOTHING I can do to be any more whole or holy, I will stop striving and straining to be perfect, and trust You to keep me until that great and glorious day when You come or call me home for the honor of Your name. Amen.

Are you trying to add anything to your faith? If you believe in the finished work Jesus has done for you on the cross, there is absolutely nothing you can add. In Christ, you are complete, circumcised, buried, raised, alive, forgiven, free, and victorious! Trust Him to do what He says He will do – keep you to the end.

3

Day Three
Recreated

2 Corinthians 5:17

This means that anyone who belongs to Christ has become a new person. The old life is gone; a new life has begun!

Dearest Father in Heaven,

I BELIEVE You saved my life by deliberately removing my dysfunctional, diseased heart, and replacing it with the strong, healthy heart of Your dear Son. This new, grateful heart now beats in vital unison with Yours. Since You recreated me, I live differently by being:

R-eceptive of people who are fundamentally opposed to me
E-mpathetic and kind rather than cold and callous
C-ontent with the things You've given me, not covetous
R-ecognizant of the good in bad circumstances
E-cstatic with the truth, not depressed by deception
A-ccepting of people despite their faults, not critical or judgmental
T-olerant of abrasive people and harsh conditions
E-ven-tempered and calm, even when mistreated
D-evoted, diligent, and hopeful to the end

With a transformed heart, I'll graciously pour out compassion and love on hurting, helpless, and hopeless people as I bring glory to You through the exuberant new life You've given me in Jesus, Your Son. Amen.

What radical difference has Christ made in your life? What difference will you make in the lives of others?

Day Four

Following the Spirit

Galatians 5:25

Since we are living by the Spirit, let us follow the Spirit's leading in every part of our lives.

Father in Heaven,

I BELIEVE You graciously chose me to be Your beloved child, adopting me into Your great big diverse family when I was an utterly rebellious brat demanding my own way. For reasons I cannot fathom, You picked me and sent Your infinitely powerful Spirit to tame my wild and wicked ways.

Since I am vitally dependent on Your divine discipline to break my bad habits, I choose to relinquish control of my life to Your Spirit. Under Your wise counsel and watchful eye, I'll learn to imitate Your crazy love as I purposefully read and study my Bible. My heart will joyfully flutter and my mind will peacefully sing as I walk step by step with You through all kinds of problems and pressures.

Firmly in Your grasp of grace, I'll not only endure irritating people but also demonstrate Your undeniable loving kindness to them. Trusting You to gently lead and guide me by Your Spirit, I'll live virtuously in the midst of difficulty, drawing others to Your remarkable life changing power. Amen.

What steps do you need to take in order to walk by the Spirit?

When you keep in step with the Spirit, the outgrowth of the Spirit will be love, joy, peace, patience, kindness, goodness, faithfulness, gentleness and self-control (Galatians 5:22-23).

Day Five

Exercising the Spirit

1 Timothy 4:8

Physical training is good, but training for godliness is much better,
promising benefits in this life and in the life to come.

Jesus,

I BELIEVE You are my Divine Coach and Trainer. I am weak, out of shape and ready to get rid of unnecessary stress and strain in my life. I desire to get firm and fit with You. I know Your fitness program will be challenging, painful and expensive; but the end result will be well worth it. Willingly, I'm surrendering my entire life to You, determined to improve my image from the inside out.

Focused on You, I'll discover what it really means to follow You. As my heart beats in rapid unity with Yours, I'll breathe in Your sensational power and blow out Your super natural strength. Refreshing Living Water from my Bible will revitalize my soul. As I monitor my heart and measure my progress, the visible lifetime benefits will motivate me to keep moving with You. As I become firm and fit in my faith I will develop the stamina to endure everyday problems and pressures. Others will recognize the drastic improvement in my character and praise Your glorious name. Amen.

What will you do to get firm and fit with Jesus? Even if you spend as little as 10 minutes a day focused on Him, it will benefit you spiritually. Find a study buddy and commit to working out together by doing a daily reading together. Share with each other what the Lord is teaching you. Together, you'll encourage each other to grow in His strength.

Losing Weight

Matthew 11:28-30

Then Jesus said, "Come to me, all of you who are weary and carry heavy burdens, and I will give you rest. Take my yoke upon you. Let me teach you, because I am humble and gentle at heart, and you will find rest for your souls. For my yoke is easy to bear, and the burden I give you is light."

Jesus,

I BELIEVE You are my heavenly health Coach. I come to You worn down and burned out. Constant problems and pressure have packed on the pounds. I'm weighed down with worries, bulging with burdens, and full of fear. I don't want to spend the rest of my life feeling lousy! I want to lose my pounds of problems Your way!

Actively using my Bible, I'll consume reasonable portions of strength enhancing nutrients. Vigorously working through Your Word will stimulate my messed up mind. Coupled with the power of persistent prayer and praise, my problems will dissipate as I transfer their weight to You.

Under Your gentle control my heart and mind will miraculously heal. Resting on Your promises I will achieve my lifelong goal of being shaped into Your extraordinary image. In my life, Lord, be magnified so that I can be more productive for You. Amen.

Consider giving the weight of your worries to Jesus. He's inviting you to "Come!" Work out with Him. He's offering to take your load and teach you to live differently. As you trust Him with your heart problems, the physical ones may dissipate too.

Give your burdens to the Lord and he will take care of you. Psalm 55:22

Day Seven

Slow Down & Live

Psalm 130:5-6

I am counting on the Lord;
yes, I am counting on him.
I have put my hope in his word.
I long for the Lord
more than sentries long for the dawn,
yes, more than sentries long for the dawn.

Holy Father,

Even though I BELIEVE You promise special blessings for those who quietly wait, it's very difficult for me! I'm living in a fast-paced world where we drive fast cars through fast food restaurants, gobbling the grub as we speed down the freeway. Instant cash at ATM's and instant information on the internet provide instant gratification. And I wonder why waiting is hard!

At break-neck speed my perception is poor and my vision distorted as in the darkness of night. Going at a slower, safer speed I begin to see Your immense golden goodness. I come to utterly depend on You for power, provision and protection. I learn to trust Your principles, promises and purposes. Concentrating on Your goodness, I find peace and hope in Your Word, the Bible.

Please clothe me with the patience of Christ to endure the long, silent night of my soul, eagerly expecting the definitive morning when the Son will rise and warm my heart with hope, peace and everlasting happiness. Amen.

What are you waiting for? Are you devising your own schemes and plans to get ahead? I encourage you to slow down and go with God. In His Word you will find the only Way to true peace and everlasting happiness… but His way is not usually fast, nor instantaneous!

Day Eight

Living Intentionally

Psalm 39:4-5

Lord, remind me how brief my time on earth will be.
Remind me that my days are numbered—
how fleeting my life is.
You have made my life no longer than the width of my hand.
My entire lifetime is just a moment to you;
at best, each of us is but a breath.

Heavenly Father,

I BELIEVE You are the epic Creator of all living things. Thank You for the fabulous, fragile gift of life. I will cherish every day as a valuable present from You, my loving Father. Forgive me for tossing miracle moments aside to worry about insignificant incidences. Often I spend more time securing my life on earth, than I do thinking about where I will spend eternity.

Life is short! I know not the length of my sojourn here on earth. As I spend time reading my Bible, marinate my mind in Your astonishing mercy. Saturate my heart with Your outlandish grace. Then, when the heat of trials is turned up, I'll be flavored with rich faith that emanates peace, hope, and joy.

Rain or shine, this is a perfect day made by You for my pleasure. Living in the blessing of each precious moment, I'll cheerfully love and serve others because today could be my last chance. Please just give me more of Jesus so that I will focus on the most important matters today – the matters of Your heart, for Your kingdom. Amen.

You just don't know when your life will be interrupted by an unexpected tragedy. Resolve to live each day like it's your last. Take advantage of every opportunity to tell someone you love them and that Jesus does too! Tomorrow may be too late.

Day Nine

Exercising Hospitably

1 Peter 4:9

Cheerfully share your home with those who need a meal or a place to stay.

Father in Heaven -

I BELIEVE in the miracle of a Christian home. My home is not my own. It belongs to You. Often the details of entertaining consume me. I want to impress people with my meticulously well-kept house, my clever decorating, and my gourmet cooking. I am so busy with the preparations that I forget WHO I am serving.

Empower me to value people above things. Instead of putting away the dirt, help me to put away my pride and allow others to see my humanness. Shape my home into a place free of false pretenses where people can relax and be themselves.

Open my heart to someone in need of healing and rest. I will gladly share my home with them. It is my desire to use the gifts You've lavished on me to glorify You. I am Your humble servant. Please show me how to practice biblical hospitality that honors You. Amen.

The root word of hospitality is "hospital." Hospitals are places to rest and heal. Our homes should be places where people can come to rest and heal. Think of your home as a hospital. Consider inviting to your home: the elderly neighbor who is always alone, the family that just received devastating news, or a newcomer to your community.

Day Ten
Content in Christ

1 Timothy 6: 6-8

Yet true godliness with contentment is itself great wealth. After all, we brought nothing with us when we came into the world, and we can't take anything with us when we leave it. So if we have enough food and clothing, let us be content.

Life Giving God,

I BELIEVE You are the Creator, Owner and Giver of everything! I'm exceedingly thankful for your incredible provision! You have given me so much more than I need. Help me to be content with what I have. It's difficult to flee from the advertising-induced need for every new gadget and gizmo. In a materialistic world, distinguishing between wants and needs is tough. Teach me by Your Spirit to live a genuinely simple life and find fulfillment in fewer belongings. I want to be rich in faith, hope and love.

All too often I take for granted the spectacular mysteries of life and fail to recognize Your abundant provision. The vast beauty, splendor and majesty of creation are always there for me to enjoy. Family and friends are irreplaceable blessings to cherish and protect. Best of all, You've given me the priceless gift of eternal life through Your Son. I have so much more than food and clothing to be thankful for!

Rather than chasing after meaningless possessions, I long to pursue a satisfying life of wonder. I long to consistently do what's right and pleasing to You, the One who daily enriches me with amazing grace and everlasting love. Amen.

How can you simplify your life in order to do what's right and pleases God?

11

Matthew 6: 19-21

Jesus commanded: "Don't store up treasures here on earth, where moths eat them and rust destroys them, and where thieves break in and steal. Store your treasures in heaven, where moths and rust cannot destroy, and thieves do not break in and steal. Wherever your treasure is, there the desires of your heart will also be.

My Jesus,

I BELIEVE I have everything I need in You. You are the most valuable Treasure of all time!

Foolishly, I've invested my money in worthless possessions, accumulating assets that can be destroyed in a heartbeat. My warm and cozy home is full of trite trinkets that can easily be taken by a thief. Blessed with an overabundance of food, I'm never hungry. I've spent a small fortune on a wonderful wardrobe that I wash, wear and waste. Forgive me, Father, for overindulging in useless pleasures when others are just looking for a simple roof over their head, begging for a mere morsel to eat, and wearing my worn out wardrobe.

Because my heart and all I own belong to You, make me profoundly generous. When You touch my pocketbook with Your love, I will readily open my wallet to make a secure investment in Your kingdom. In return, You've promised me the everlasting riches of Your glorious name. Amen.

Thank God for all that He's given you. Consider all the ways you extravagantly spend money on unnecessary items while others struggle to survive. Out of heartfelt gratitude, resolve to be more generous and find someone to share your wealth with today.

12

Day Twelve
Trusting God

Luke 12: 22-23

Then, turning to his disciples, Jesus said, "I tell you not to worry about everyday life—whether you have enough food to eat or enough clothes to wear. For life is more than food, and your body more than clothing.

Jesus,

I BELIEVE You tenderly teach me hard lessons. Every day I worry about unimportant things. I should be more concerned with where I'll spend eternity, what I feed my mind, and the condition of my heart. Today if I pass by a field of flowers, I will gaze with wonder on their fabulous form. They do not shop or primp; yet, they look stunning.

Lord, I long to believe that I'm more valuable than flowers that are here today and gone tomorrow. Rather than worrying about my life, help me to live in Your presence where I'll realize the magnitude of Your love, believing You will take care of all my needs one day at a time.

Devoting my attention to what You're doing at the moment, I won't get worked up about the future. When tough times come, I'll trust You to sustain me for the glory of Your life-giving name. Amen.

What temporal things are you worried about? What do you gain from worrying about these things? When you appear before God's throne He's going to examine your heart. Feed on His power-packed promises. Clothe yourself in righteousness, humility and love from the armoire of God. Then, you'll have nothing to worry about because you'll look and feel splendid.

13

Day Thirteen
Clothed in Mercy

Matthew 9:13

*Jesus said, "Now go and learn the meaning of this Scripture: 'I want
you to show mercy, not offer sacrifices.' For I have come to call not
those who think they are righteous, but those who know they are
sinners."*

Merciful Father -

I BELIEVE You love, chose, and adopted me despite my indecent lifestyle, impure motives, and improper attitudes. Mercifully accepting a rabble-rouser like me, You brought me into Your heavenly workshop and gave me beautiful new eyes that recognize society's scoundrels as lost and lonely souls. With Your perspective, I am able to see divine possibilities in colorful characters.

Father, forgive me for being more concerned about my rituals, routines, and reputation than I am about restoring relationships. It's not about ME. It's all about YOU. Please enlarge my heart and fill it with more of Your matchless mercy, love and grace. Show me someone who needs a touch of Your greatness today. I will graciously lavish them with the same life-changing mercy, love and grace You pour out on me and bring honor to Your name. Amen.

Who are the despised "tax collectors" and sinners in your life that need a touch from the merciful hand of Jesus? Look beyond their questionable standard of living and include them in your activities where they may encounter Your Savior.

God says three times in His Word, "I desire mercy, not sacrifice." Matthew 9:13, 12:7 and Hosea 6:6. He doesn't want our rituals and routines! He wants our relationship! And, when our hearts are full of Him, we'll notice the lost and lonely souls around us and be compelled to show compassion.

Day Fourteen

Bearing Fruit

Isaiah 32:15-18

Until at last the Spirit is poured out
on us from heaven.
Then the wilderness will become a fertile field,
and the fertile field will yield bountiful crops.
Justice will rule in the wilderness
and righteousness in the fertile field.
And this righteousness will bring peace.
Yes, it will bring quietness and confidence forever.
My people will live in safety, quietly at home.
They will be at rest.

Holy Spirit,

I BELIEVE You are the River of Life. Gush over me! Water the wasteland of my heart with Your marvelous grace. Carry away the awful debris from my past. In the swift current of Your sparkling love, restore my reputation. Then, swell up in my soul like a spring in the desert.

Flow over the badland of my mind, and cultivate it into a fertile field. Plant in it the good seed of Your Word. Tend to me patiently, teaching me to grow Your way. Raise me up to produce spiritually sweet succulent fruit. Rooted in You, others will notice the beauty of Your quiet peace and confidence growing in me.

In Your presence, I'll calmly rest, trusting You to protect me from the prickly weeds of proud, power-hungry people who threaten to disturb my peace. Under Your tender loving care, I'll live a secure, serene and satisfied life, while consistently making right choices that bless Your holy and righteous name. Amen.

Ask the Holy Spirit to search your heart and show you the damage caused by poor choices. Humbly acknowledge your mistakes. Sit quietly, still before Him, allowing His Spirit to wash over You. Refreshed by the River of Life, you will receive the rich rewards of peace, quietness, and confidence forever.

No Excuse

Romans 2: 1

You may think you can condemn such people, but you are just as bad, and you have no excuse! When you say they are wicked and should be punished, you are condemning yourself, for you who judge others do these very same things.

Holy Father,

I BELIEVE You are the only Righteous Judge. Forgive me for donning Your robe, stepping behind Your desk, and pounding down Your gavel to announce the "guilty" verdict. I am just as bad as those I condemn.

How can I judge a book when the chapters aren't completely written? You author every story and uniquely craft each ending.

I think of the thief dying on the cross next to You. In the last paragraph of his life story, he acknowledged You, asking You to remember him in Paradise. In the end, You pounded the gavel and proclaimed him "not guilty", assuring him a place in Your kingdom. While the watching world convicted him, You patiently pardoned him. Your outrageous kindness and scandalous mercy is astonishing! Teach me, Your Honor, to bear with others to the very end for Your name's sake. Amen.

God is the Father of many chances. He bears with us, holding back His judgment, allowing us time to change our mind. Likewise, He wants us to bear with others. Talk to God about who you need to show mercy today. Then, step aside, remove the robe, put down the gavel and let Him announce the verdict. He alone is worthy.

16

Day Sixteen
Clothed in Humility

John 13: 14-15

Jesus said to them, "And since I, your Lord and Teacher, have washed your feet, you ought to wash each other's feet. I have given you an example to follow. Do as I have done to you."

Jesus, My Lord and Teacher,

I BELIEVE You reign in power with full authority over heaven and earth. Yet You left Your glorious celestial home, took off Your crown, set aside Your power, and laid down Your glory to became fully human and homeless to teach me Your ways.

Thank You for stooping down to wash filthy feet in order to show me how to humbly serve You and others. If You, the Darling of Heaven, can take on the unappealing task of washing muddy feet, then who am I to stand around watching and waiting for someone else to do the dirty work? Clothe me with humility and a willing spirit to…

> S-hamelessly stoop down to do unpleasant tasks
>
> E-agerly serve others even when it's untimely
>
> R-isk my reputation to touch the unattractive
>
> V-alue human beings
>
> E-xpress Your love to its fullest extent

With all my heart I want to be like Jesus. Open my eyes to see who I can serve today. Out of love and respect, I will do whatever You ask to honor Your extraordinarily humble name. Amen

Intentionally look for someone to humbly serve today.

Luke 10: 30-37

Jesus said:"A Jewish man was traveling from Jerusalem down to Jericho, and he was attacked by bandits. They stripped him of his clothes, beat him up, and left him half dead beside the road. By chance a priest came along. But when he saw the man lying there, he crossed to the other side of the road and passed him by. A Temple assistant walked over and looked at him lying there, but he also passed by on the other side. Then a despised Samaritan came along, and when he saw the man, he felt compassion for him. Going over to him, the Samaritan soothed his wounds with olive oil and wine and bandaged them. Then he put the man on his own donkey and took him to an inn, where he took care of him The next day he handed the innkeeper two silver coins, telling him, 'Take care of this man. If his bill runs higher than this, I'll pay you the next time I'm here.'

"Now which of these three would you say was a neighbor to the man who was attacked by bandits?" Jesus asked.

The man replied, "The one who showed him mercy."

Then Jesus said, "Yes, now go and do the same."

Jesus, You are the Perfect Teacher!

I BELIEVE You are graciously compassionate! Thank you for teaching me that my neighbors are the people around me who have been stripped of their dignity. Beaten down by problems and pressures, their spirits are left to die disgracefully.

Forgive me for all the times I've:

> H-urt someone and walked away like the bandit
>
> U-nkindly passed by someone suffering because of my arrogance like the religious leaders
>
> R-easoned my lack of love by standing around and talking about it like the experts in the law
>
> T-ried to capitalize on a bad situation like the innkeeper

Teach me to be unabashedly merciful like the Samaritan who was the least respected among all these men, yet had the biggest heart. Please remove the calluses from my own heart, and the scales from my eyes so that I will see the injured souls around me today. By Your grace, I will stop and nurse their wounds no matter the cost. With corrected vision, I will see interruptions as divine opportunities to show Your love to people in distress. May mercy flow like a river through me because of Your amazing love. Amen.

Look for a disgraced person with whom you can share the love of Christ in a practical way today whether it's convenient or not.

18

Day Eighteen
A Living Bible

Philippians 3:17

Dear brothers and sisters, pattern your lives after mine, and learn from those who follow our example.

Jesus,

I BELIEVE You are the Perfect Pattern for godly living. I long to model my life after Yours.

As I study my Bible, enlighten me with understanding of Your precepts and principles. By Your Spirit, enliven me to obey You. With Your Words, in all their richness, alive in me, I'll accurately represent the kingdom of heaven on earth. Love and patience will show my strong faith. Peace will reign in my heart. Praise and thanksgiving will always be on my lips. My kindness and humility will give others an honest impression of You.

Please send godly people into my life so that I can see biblical principles in practice. Seeing others imitating You helps me grow in Your likeness. Hearing them tell about Your work in their lives inspires me to persevere. As I study Your Word and watch others, I'll become a living Bible, persuading and motivating others to bring glory, honor and fame to You. Amen.

What impression do people have of Christ when they see or talk with you? What changes do you need to make in your life to honor Him?

As Christians, we are to represent Christ. When those around us say, "I didn't know you were a Christian," we have failed to represent Him as we should. We are not merely Christ followers; we are His ambassadors. (2 Corinthians 5:20)

19 Day Nineteen
Time to Unwind

Isaiah 58:13-14

"Keep the Sabbath day holy.

Don't pursue your own interests on that day,
but enjoy the Sabbath

and speak of it with delight as the Lord's holy day.
Honor the Sabbath in everything you do on that day,

and don't follow your own desires or talk idly.
Then the Lord will be your delight.

I will give you great honor
and satisfy you with the inheritance I promised to your ancestor Jacob.

I, the Lord, have spoken!"

Lord of the Sabbath,

I BELIEVE You are the designer of the day of rest! Forgive me for neglecting this provision and command. You know my stress and my need for time away from the usual routine.

You Yourself set the pace by working hard for six days to make the entire universe. Then, You stopped and enjoyed the fruit of Your labor. My problem is my perception that my work never ends. I keep going and going and going, until all of my energy's zapped and there's zilch left for You, my family or me.

Enable me by Your Spirit to intentionally make time to unwind. Away from the insanity, I'll discover ineffable peace and joy. Free from craziness, my weary soul will welcome the calm. A revived heart, re-energized Spirit, and renewed strength will be my rich reward. Well rested, I'll consistently make right choices that bring glory to Your name. My vibrant life will draw others to You, the perfect designer of the day of rest. Amen.

The Lord has commanded, "Keep the Sabbath day holy!" To disobey is to dishonor the Lord of the Sabbath. For one month, intentionally keep every Sunday open. Take a nap. Read a book. Take a walk. Play games. Visit the sick or elderly. It's a difficult discipline, but you'll notice a decisive difference in your demeanor and begin longing for that weekly day of rest.

Building Bridges

Daniel 1: 3-4, 17, 19

Then the king ordered Ashpenaz, his chief of staff, to bring to the palace some of the young men of Judah's royal family and other noble families, who had been brought to Babylon as captives. "Select only strong, healthy, and good-looking young men," he said. "Make sure they are well versed in every branch of learning, are gifted with knowledge and good judgment, and are suited to serve in the royal palace. Train these young men in the language and literature of Babylon."

God gave these four young men an unusual aptitude for understanding every aspect of literature and wisdom. And God gave Daniel the special ability to interpret the meanings of visions and dreams..

The king talked with them, and no one impressed him as much as Daniel, Hananiah, Mishael, and Azariah. So they entered the royal service.

Most High King of Heaven,

I BELIEVE You handpicked and adopted me into Your royal family despite my squalid choices. With my deformities and degradation vanquished at the cross, You make me virtuous, lavish me with wisdom and knowledge, and qualify me to serve You on earth.

This world is not my home. My home is in heaven. I am a foreigner in a strange place. The wholesome language I speak is uncommon here. The Christian literature I'm familiar with is abnormal. Help me adapt to the community where I live, work and play.

Give me a courageous heart and determined mind to follow You beyond my perceived limits; beyond the pleasant walls and protection of my church to unprincipled people in need of a Savior. Clinging to my faith and trusting in Your power, I'll inform people of the truth about You in words they'll understand. By developing meaningful relationships and clear communication, I'll build bridges that connect them to Your glorious kingdom for the praise of Your name. Amen.

You don't have to go to another land to learn a new language. Study the culture in your community in order to understand its values and traditions. Then, find and begin interacting with a non-churched group. Reputable community service organizations need to be influenced by the Kingdom too.

21

Day Twenty-one
Holy and Whole

1 Thessalonians 5:23-24

Now may the God of peace make you holy in every way, and may your whole spirit and soul and body be kept blameless until our Lord Jesus Christ comes again. God will make this happen, for he who calls you is faithful.

Holy God of Peace,

I BELIEVE Your powerful promise. Blessed assurance! You will make me holy and whole. Gripped by Your power I can:

Be cheerful in all circumstances because I know You have reserved a place for me at the Wedding Feast of the Lamb.

Keep an open line of communication with You by living every moment of life in the grip of Your grace.

Be grateful in the midst of misery because no matter what happens here on earth when the role is called up yonder I'll be there.

Fuel the fire in my heart with Your Word until I'm fully absorbed and blazing with Your glory.

Humbly receive instructions, exhortations, and warnings from the godly men and women You put in my life.

Examine everything carefully, keep only what's good, and toss out anything tainted with evil.

Spirit of the Living God, I delight to do Your will. Keep me strong to the end so my whole heart, mind, and soul will be blameless on the day You return. All glory to You my great God and King forever and ever. Amen.

Can you think of any area of your life you are withholding from God? Be honest with yourself. God already knows. Resolve to live blamelessly.

Living Like Christ

2 Peter 1:5-8

In view of all this, make every effort to respond to God's promises. Supplement your faith with a generous provision of moral excellence, and moral excellence with knowledge, and knowledge with self-control, and self-control with patient endurance, and patient endurance with godliness, and godliness with brotherly affection, and brotherly affection with love for everyone.

The more you grow like this, the more productive and useful you will be in your knowledge of our Lord Jesus Christ.

Father,

I BELIEVE You called me by Your goodness and grace to personally know You and Your divine power. I BELIEVE that through Your exceedingly great and precious promises I have everything I need to reflect Your virtues and avoid the desirous devices of the devil. By Your Spirit, supplement my faith with

> A generous measure of moral excellence
> A double dose of knowledge
> A substantial quantity of self-control
> A massive portion of patient endurance
> A heaping helping of holiness
> A basketful of brotherly kindness
> *And*, an abundant allowance of love for everyone

You promise if I possess these Christ-like characteristics in increasing portions, I will be prosperous and productive in knowledge and service to You. Lord, with all my heart I want to fall in love with Your genuine goodness. Don't let me be deceived by the ways of the world, but prepare me to spend eternity praising You in Paradise for the sake of Your good name. Amen.

God wants to produce His character in us, but it won't happen without our cooperation and effort. If you want to be fruitful and useful, remain in the Word, cooperate with God, and make every effort to be like Christ. Your actions will show what You know about Him.

23 *Day Twenty-three*
Clothed in Goodness

2 Thessalonians 1:11-12

So we keep on praying for you, asking our God to enable you to live a life worthy of his call. May he give you the power to accomplish all the good things your faith prompts you to do. Then the name of our Lord Jesus will be honored because of the way you live, and you will be honored along with him. This is all made possible because of the grace of our God and Lord, Jesus Christ.

God of Goodness and Grace,

I BELIEVE that one day, quite possibly soon, You will be revealed in the sky in an incredible blaze of glory and call me to come heavenward with You. What a day of rejoicing that will be!

While I wait for Your glorious appearance, I want to live a life worthy of Your call. Your plans are far superior to mine. Enlighten me by Your Spirit to recognize my unique purpose, and embolden me to take positive steps to accomplish it. Clothed in Your goodness and grace I will honor You by my faithful work, my loving deeds, and my enduring hope in Jesus Christ—all, of course, made possible by Your Spirit living in me.

With quiet confidence and holy joy I eagerly anticipate that bright and blessed day when Your adoring angels will transport me with eternal rapture into Paradise, a place of undeserved privilege where I will live happily-ever-after with You because of Jesus, the One and Only. Amen.

Are you anticipating the day when Jesus appears in a blaze of glory to call you home eternally? If so, pray the prayer of Paul and ask Him to enable you to live a life worthy of His call. Recognize your unique purpose and take positive steps to accomplish it to bring honor and glory to the God of goodness and grace.

24 Day Twenty-four
My Heart, Christ's Home

1 Chronicles 22:19

Now seek the Lord your God with all your heart and soul. Build the sanctuary of the Lord God so that you can bring the Ark of the Lord's Covenant and the holy vessels of God into the Temple built to honor the Lord's name.

Father in Heaven,

I BELIEVE Your love and faithfulness are inexhaustible. Because You love me beyond the limits of my imagination, I'm compelled to live a life of love, personally and passionately devoted to You.

Please search the temple of my heart and show me anything that I love more than You. By Your power and grace, remove those obstacles in order to build a sacred place of honor and worship for Your priceless precepts, principles, and promises.

Even as I am filled with Your vast riches, I am overpowered by Your love which drives me to follow Your lead. The closer I get to You, the easier it becomes to identify the people and purposes that matter most to You. Living in pure, uninterrupted devotion to You, my spontaneous actions and positive attitudes will please You and encourage those around me.

More than anything else in the world, I desire to worship You ceaselessly in the temple of my heart where Your precious treasure abounds because of my commitment to Jesus—and His to me. Amen.

Because of God's inexhaustible love and enduring faithfulness, are you willing to pour out your life for Him? Identify those things in your life that prevent you from just being with Him. Then determine to give Him the first fruit of your time each morning for Bible study and prayer.

25

Day Twenty-five
Clothed in Christ

Colossians 3:12-14

Since God chose you to be the holy people whom he loves, you must clothe yourselves with tenderhearted mercy, kindness, humility, gentleness, and patience. You must make allowance for each other's faults and forgive the person who offends you. Remember, the Lord forgave you, so you must forgive others. And the most important piece of clothing you must wear is love. Love is what binds us all together in perfect harmony.

Holy God ~

I BELIEVE You chose me to be Your beloved, holy child and raised me to a vibrant new life with Christ. With my eyes fixed on the realities of heaven, I want to intentionally focus more on my glorious future than the divisive vices of this earth. With my mind set on You, I will strip off my wicked worldly ways in order to put on the eye-catching qualities of Christ.

Before I go out of the house each day, please dress me in tenderhearted mercy, kindness, humility, gentleness and patience. Clothe me with an even temper and quickness to forgive. Bundled up in the all-important overcoat of LOVE I will exude grace and gratefulness.

Clothed in Your radiant righteousness, my boldness and brilliance will shine in the darkness and difficult moments. I want people to notice Your energizing power within me and praise Your holy name. Amen.

Take off your bad behaviors and despicable deeds and put on the eye-catching, radiant righteousness of Christ. People will be drawn to your unusual accouterments and thank God for your presence in their life.

Day Twenty-six
Live Wisely

Colossians 4:5-6

Live wisely among those who are not believers, and make the most of every opportunity. Let your conversation be gracious and attractive so that you will have the right response for everyone.

Gracious, Jesus,

I BELIEVE You lived and walked on this earth to show me the way to live wisely among non-believers. Far from Your heavenly home, in a world of hateful, hostile people, You were not cold but compassionate, not gruff but gentle, not resentful but righteous, not haughty but humble, not fearsome but forgiving.

While I am still in this dark world far from my eternal home, I must live wisely and make the most of every opportunity to tell people about You. People who die today without knowing You will face infinity in the inferno of hell, forever separated from Your goodness and grace. You are the One who saves, the One and Only Way to an everlasting vivacious life.

Please give me Your beautiful heart for the lost and the courage to exercise Your all-consuming power that is within me to share the Good News clearly and compassionately. Because You have shown me kindness, patience, and true love, I will graciously, tenderly, and effectively share it with others through my words and conduct for the sake of Your life-saving, life-giving name. Amen.

What will you do to live wisely, making the most of every opportunity to represent the Kingdom of Heaven on earth today? There is a world full of lost people who will spend eternity in Hell if someone doesn't tell them about Jesus.

27 Day Twenty-seven

Exercise Grace

Isaiah 52:7

How beautiful on the mountains
*   are the feet of the messenger who brings good news,*
the good news of peace and salvation,
*   the news that the God of Israel reigns!*

God of Israel,

I BELIEVE You reign in glory, splendor and majesty. I long to ascend the High and Holy Mountain into Your pristine presence, but my soul is sore and swollen from sojourning through stress and strain. Trials and tribulations have taken away my stamina. I'm in dire need of a power pedicure at Your beauty bar.

Soak me in the holy and healing bath of biblical truth. Purify my sin-stung soul in the cleansing fountain of forgiveness. Scrub away the calluses that clog my heart. Buff away the burrs of bitterness that bind me. Massage my heart with the sweet fragrant oil of the Holy Spirit until it is soft and tender like Yours. In the beauty of holiness, I'll recognize that You, Lord, are the only good news in this dark and dismal world.

Blessed with beautiful feet of faith, I'll be perfectly shaped for service. Stimulated from my sweet time with You, I'll gladly exercise extravagant, exfoliating grace toward others by telling them the good news of peace and sharing the salvation of Your holy and healing name. Amen.

Spend time in the holy and healing words of your Bible allowing the Holy Spirit to give you beautiful feet of faith. Then exercise those feet by going to tell others the good news of peace and salvation.

28 Day Twenty-eight
Working Out

Philippians 2:12-13

Work hard to show the results of your salvation, obeying God with deep reverence and fear. For God is working in you, giving you the desire and the power to do what pleases him.

Heavenly Father,

I BELIEVE that I am complete in Christ Jesus; however that does not mean I can be complacent or careless. Out of deep reverence and fear, give me a sincere desire to work out my salvation so I exhibit an exhilarating life based on my belief in the work You have done for me. I eagerly hope for the day when my body will be free from sin and suffering, but even now I am assured You can use me.

I wait patiently, empowered by Your indwelling Spirit to do what pleases You. With Your help I serve You wholeheartedly—without complaining and arguing—so unbelievers get a true impression of You and the gospel that saved me. With a clear conscience, my words should be consistently positive, encouraging and uplifting. Determined to live harmoniously in Your Church, full of problematic people, I will twinkle like a star in a dark and depraved world. Holding onto and holding out the Word of Life, I seek to live a life of worth and excellence that resembles the likeness of Your name and lifts It high. Amen.

Are you shining like a bright star in this dark and depraved world, or are you grumbling and complaining? Shine out for God! Let people see your hope, joy and peace in the pitch black night as the days get ever darker.

29 Day Twenty-nine
Sweeter Than Chocolate

Psalm 34:8

Taste and see that the Lord is good.

Sweet Jesus,

I BELIEVE Your Words are sweeter than chocolate! Your delicious precepts and promises are irresistible. They satisfy my most intense cravings and evoke pleasure in the deepest parts of my soul.

Hidden in my Bible are surprising nuggets of truth. As I taste and savor each one, I discover Your mouthwatering goodness that melts my heart. Your opulent promises are my source of hope. Sinking my teeth into Your sumptuous loving kindness, my troubled spirit is comforted. Indulging in Your luxurious mercies refreshes my distressed mind. Treating myself to Your bittersweet commands makes my salvation seem all the more thick, rich and smooth.

Your Words, O Lord, are an attractive treat! They are my heart's delight and joy! I have tasted and experienced Your goodness. With all my heart I want to savor the flavor every day of my life, and share the sweetness with others to glorify and bless Your sweet name. Amen.

Enjoy the rich delicacies of God's Word. Go ahead! Taste and see that the Lord is good!

30

Day Thirty
Trusting the Lord

Proverbs 3:5-6

Trust in the Lord with all your heart;
do not depend on your own understanding.
Seek his will in all you do,
and he will show you which path to take.

All-Knowing One,

I BELIEVE You are perfect in knowledge and exalted in power. You are the Master Mind of the universe. No one can begin to grasp Your greatness. Yet, I feebly try. Every time I finagle ways to figure out where You're taking me on this journey of life, I only end up exhausted, lost and confused. Your plans are far superior and brighter and better than mine. You are always right, always good and always loving.

Please humble me, Lord Jesus, and teach me Your ways. Give me a fresh revelation of Who You are, and I will acknowledge You in all my ways. A proper perspective of You helps me trust You with all my heart and not rely on my own foolish wisdom. When I read my Bible, You light my way, make my path straight and lead me on the highway to holiness. Thank You for the guarantee that if I walk by faith, You will help me one step at a time to magnify Your great Name. Amen.

God promises to make your paths straight if you: 1) trust Him with all your heart, 2) stop relying on yourself, and 3) acknowledge Him in every decision.

The way to accomplish this is to get to know Him better and more personally. The only way to know Him is through His Word, the Bible.

31

Day Thirty-one
Jesus is Coming

Revelation 22:7, 12

"Look, I am coming soon! Blessed are those who obey the words of prophecy written in this book ... *Look, I am coming soon, bringing my reward with me to repay all people according to their deeds."*

King of Heaven,

I BELIEVE Your Word says it clearly: You are coming soon!
Glory! Hallelujah! O that I will be found worthy of Your honor.

> For my devotion, You'll endow me with the privilege of eating
> from the tree of life in the Garden of Paradise.

> For overcoming oppression, You'll award me the crown of
> everlasting life.

> For believing the truth, You'll bless me with the Bread of Life
> and a brand new name.

> For pursuing purity and peace to the very end, You'll give me
> divine authority.

> For dying to my selfish desires, You promise that I'll be worthy
> to walk with You as a winner.

> For holding onto Your precepts and promises, You'll make me a
> pillar of praise that supports Your glorious presence.

> For opening the door and welcoming You in, You'll honor me
> with a seat next to Your Majesty.

Of course, all that is good in me is tied to the powerful name of
Jesus who is coming soon and makes all things possible. Blessed
assurance! Amen.

*Ponder the rewards and recognition you will receive for obeying the words
of prophecy written to the seven churches in Revelation 2 and 3. To obtain
them, will you allow God to make adjustments to your life?*

10 Ways to Put Feet to Your Faith and Live with *Vibrancy!*

1. Be Bold. Share the Good News that Jesus saves with a lost soul.
2. Be Purposeful. Identify your God-given purposes and take positive steps to fulfill them for the glory of God.
3. Be Sensitive. Visit an elderly or disabled person. Take along a balloon bouquet to brighten their surroundings.
4. Be Helpful. Relieve weary parents of small children by occupying the children for an afternoon.
5. Be Merciful. Write letters to prisoners who have been forgotten by society. Tell them about God's forgiveness.
6. Be Prayerful. Offer to pray for someone who is hurting—and do it on the spot.
7. Be Relational. Find and begin interacting with a service group. Reputable civic organizations need Kingdom influence too.
8. Be Generous. Cut back on extravagantly spending and share your wealth with someone in need.
9. Be Hospitable. Invite to your home: the elderly neighbor who is always alone, the family that just received devastating news, or a newcomer to your community.
10. Be Expressive. Tell someone you love them and that Jesus does too. Tomorrow may be too late.